JAMES JOYCE

JAMES JOYCE
from a portrait of 1935 by JACQUES-EMILE BLANCHE
National Portrait Gallery

JAMES JOYCE

by

J. I. M. STEWART

PUBLISHED FOR
THE BRITISH COUNCIL
BY LONGMAN GROUP LTD

LONGMAN GROUP LTD
Longman House, Burnt Mill, Harlow, Essex

*Associated companies, branches and
representatives throughout the world*

*First published 1957
Revised 1960
Reprinted with minor amendments and additions to
Bibliography 1964, 1967, 1971*
© J. I. M. Stewart 1957, 1960, 1971

*Printed in Great Britain by
F. Mildner & Sons, London, EC1*

SBN 0 582 01091 8

JAMES JOYCE

I

JAMES JOYCE was born in 1882 in Dublin, where his father was sufficiently prosperous to send him to a fashionable Jesuit boarding-school, and sufficiently improvident to be virtually penniless a few years later. Partly because of the steady decline in his family's fortunes, and partly because he himself was a little disposed to fudge the evidence, it is difficult to place Joyce tidily in a social class. Virginia Woolf, distressed by the milieu of *Ulysses*, concluded that its author must be 'a self-taught working man'. Wyndham Lewis (who was educated at Rugby) makes fun of Joyce's fictional *alter ego*, Stephen Dedalus, for his anxiety to appear a gentleman. Perhaps the Joyces became shabby more pronouncedly than they remained genteel. But class consciousness is not important with Joyce as it is with the other great novelist of the age, D. H. Lawrence. Priest, artist, citizen are Joyce's categories; not gentle and simple.

Nevertheless, what may be called the Gissing aspect of his youth—the precariousness of his slender degree of privilege, the cultural poverty of life around him—marked him deeply. He grew up arrogant and aloof, contemptuous of all proposals, whether political or artistic, for the regeneration of his country, proud of his precocious knowledge of contemporary continental literature. He renounced the Catholic Church, and in 1904 he left Ireland for good, taking with him a girl called Nora Barnacle whom he subsequently married. Miss Barnacle was not literary, but a certain pungency attends some of her recorded utterances. 'I guess the man's a genius', she said of Joyce, 'but what a dirty mind he has, hasn't he?' At least she had found a good husband and a devoted father of two children. To support his family Joyce laboured for many years as a teacher of English in

Trieste and Zürich; it was only during his later life, when benefactions and his first substantial royalties enabled him to maintain a modest establishment in Paris, that the threat of destitution ceased to hang over him. He appears to have been very sure of his genius. He resisted the discouragements of poverty, neglect, moral censorship, and a grave disease of the eyes. By the time he died in 1941 there was little responsible literary opinion in either Europe or America that failed to acknowledge him as one of the most significant writers of the age. At the same time he attracted much foolish adulation, and his books suffered (what they certainly invite) much extravagant exegesis.

II

The first of Joyce's works to appear in book form was *Chamber Music*, a collection of thirty-six short poems. It was completed in 1904 but had to wait three years for a publisher, and in the interval Joyce ceased to feel much regard for it. There is nothing surprising in this. His life's task if abundantly egotistical was wholly serious, a presenting of himself and his immediate environment to the world in fictions laying claim to the highest representative significance. With that task, to which he had already addressed himself in the apparently unpublishable *Dubliners*, the poems in *Chamber Music* have nothing to do. They are serious only in a restricted aesthetic sense, which Joyce's genius transcended from the first. He had read Elizabethan lyrics with attention, and his own verses may best be described as consummate imitations of the older poets as they appeared through a *fin de siècle* haze. They are unchallengeably lyrical; like the best of the Elizabethan, each seems to sigh for its accordant air:

Who goes amid the green wood
  With springtide all adorning her?
Who goes amid the merry green wood
  To make it merrier?

Who passes in the sunlight
  By ways that know the light footfall?
Who passes in the sweet sunlight
  With mien so virginal?

The range is narrow, and one would never guess that these
elegant dabblings and paddlings in familiar shallows pre-
luded some of the farthest voyages ever achieved over the
wide waters of the word.

Yet of poetry when sufficiently broadly defined, all
Joyce's work was to be full. From Stephen Dedalus's early
turnings-over of words—'a day of dappled seaborne clouds'
—on to the last cadence of *Finnegans Wake*—

There's where. First. We pass through grass behush the bush to.
Whish! A gull. Gulls. Far calls. Coming, far! End here. Us then. Finn,
again! Take. Bussoftlhee, mememormee! Till thousendsthee. Lps. The
keys to. Given! A way a lone a last a loved a long the

—we hear this poetry plainly; and Joyce's own readings
from his work as preserved on gramophone records are
astonishing achievements in verbal music. Moreover his
prose is 'poetic' in more ways than this. When Stephen is
looking out from the Martello tower at the beginning of
Ulysses we read:

Woodshadows floated silently by through the morning peace from
the stairhead seaward where he gazed. Inshore and farther out the mirror
of water whitened, spurned by lightshod hurrying feet. White breast of
the dim sea. The twining stresses, two by two. A hand plucking the
harpstrings merging their twining chords. Wavewhite wedded words
shimmering on the dim tide.

This is consciously presented as poetry; and it is challeng-
ingly, not fortuitously, that it comes immediately after a
quotation from Yeats. But we are not merely charmed by
a cadence. Why—we find ourselves asking—'wavewhite
wedded words'? Joyce is concerned with language as
language; he is never solely concerned with melopaeic effect.
Modern criticism has taught us to recognize in linguistic
compressions and ambiguities a range of resources characteristic of poetry proper. At its most effective, Joyce's developed
prose was to combine musical suggestion with a hitherto
unexampled power effectively to scramble the connotations
of words. In *Finnegans Wake* there is a sort of prayer for the
River Liffey that runs: 'haloed be her eve, her singtime sung,
her rill be run, unhemmed as it is uneven!'—thus echoing,
enchantingly if profanely, the Lord's Prayer: 'Hallowed be
Thy Name. Thy kingdom come. Thy will be done in earth.
As it is in heaven.' It is reasonable to believe that Joyce's
peculiar prose has been responsible for a good deal of modern
poetry, and for some reinterpretation of older poetry as well.
At least it is the work of a writer notably in command of
instruments which the present age in particular has considered a large part of the essential endowment of the poet.
Yet when Joyce addressed himself, quite simply, to metrical
composition, all his largeness and boldness left him. *Pomes
Penyeach*, the self-consciously depreciatory title of a volume
diminutive to the point of affectation which he published
in 1927, shows a mild technical development in consonance
with the ideas of the Imagists, and is the better—as so
much of the century's poetry is the better—from the
writer's acquaintance with Mr Ezra Pound. But the poet's
properties remain grey, wan, pale, frail and *démodé*:

> The moon's greygolden meshes make
> All night a veil,
> The shorelamps in the sleeping lake
> Laburnum tendrils trail.

The sly reeds whisper to the night
A name—her name—
And all my soul is a delight,
A swoon of shame.

When these lines were written *Ulysses* was well under way.

III

Exiles, a play written in 1914 or 1915, is another work of minor interest. Striking as is Joyce's lifelong obsession with Dublin and Dubliners, he was determinedly and from the first a European before he was an Irishman, and in Ibsen he found an international figure who could be held up to point a contrast with the provinciality, as he conceived it, of the Irish literary movement. But *Exiles* is not merely a counter-blast, opposing to the theatre of Yeats and Synge and Lady Gregory an aggressively naturalistic dramatic convention. It is the work of a writer who owns a real if limited temperamental affinity with Ibsen; and it contrives to treat, at once with a bleak painful intensity and a large measure of obscurity, a theme very much from the world of *A Doll's House* and *Hedda Gabler*. We are certainly shown, in one cautious commentator's words, 'a puzzling series of dilemmas concerning the limits of freedom, the demands of love, and the possessiveness inherent in marriage'. And it seems probable that Joyce proposed to give us something yet closer to Ibsen than this, the spectacle of a harsh ethical absolutism at work in a fatally egotistical personality.

Richard Rowan is an Irish writer who has lived abroad for a number of years with Bertha, a simple and unintellectual girl whom he has been unable or indisposed to marry. They return to Dublin where an old friend, Robert Hand, is determined that Rowan shall be appointed to a chair of romance literature. But Hand is also determined to seduce

Bertha; and presently we find, in a scene of neat theatrical surprise, that Bertha, while passively accepting the successive stages of this advance and even accepting an assignation with Hand, is regularly reporting the developing situation to Rowan. Rowan will not in any degree bind, guide or support her. He imagines her dead and says to Hand:

> I will reproach myself then for having taken all for myself because I would not suffer her to give to another what was hers and not mine to give, because I accepted from her her loyalty and made her life poorer in love. That is my fear. That I stand between her and any moments of life that should be hers, between her and you, between her and anyone, between her and anything. I will not do it. I cannot and I will not. I dare not.

We are shown Bertha presenting again her former passive face to Hand's eventual wooing in his secluded cottage, and then the curtain descends at an ambiguous moment. In the last act Bertha returns to Rowan with an earnest protestation that she has been true to him. But he declares that he now has a deep, deep wound of doubt in his soul, and that this wound tires him. 'He stretches himself out wearily along the lounge' and the play closes upon Bertha murmuring a passionate prayer for the return of their earliest days as lovers.

The characters in *Exiles* are very poorly realized. Rowan is represented as a lover, but seems not to have the stuff of a lover in him. He constantly demands that he himself be understood, seen for what he is and so accepted. But he virtually denies that a beloved, or any other person, is knowable. And he never himself contrives to notice this contradiction. We thus feel him to be the projection of a serious but imperfect self-analysis; and this feeling is fatal to any impression of a fullness of dramatic life. A small indication of the extent to which Joyce was here self-absorbed and self-tormented as he worked is the early percolation into the play of talk about Rowan's dead mother and the fact or calumny of his having in some way slighted her. This has no relevance to the action, and is a spill-over from Joyce's more openly autobiographical writing in the history of Dedalus.

IV

If the intellectual and emotional pressures which bore upon the young Joyce neither inform his poetry nor fortify his play, they are brought under fruitful artistic control in *Dubliners*. When eventually published in 1914, this volume contained fifteen sketches or short stories, about which Joyce had written thus to a prospective publisher nine years before:

> My intention was to write a chapter of the moral history of my country and I chose Dublin for the scene because the city seemed to me the centre of paralysis. I have tried to present it to the indifferent public under four of its aspects: childhood, adolescence, maturity and public life. The stories are arranged in this order. I have written it for the most part in a style of scrupulous meanness and with the conviction that he is a very bold man who dares to alter in the presentment, still more to deform, whatever he has seen and heard.

This is a little manifesto of naturalism; but its most significant phrase is 'moral history'. And we are not far advanced in *Dubliners* before we realize that Joyce does not differ from other young writers in having as his chief stock-in-trade a set of powerful moral responses before the spectacle of fallen humanity. It is urged upon us that almost every aspect of Dublin life is pitiful or degraded, and that to the effective asserting of this the artist must bend all his cunning. Joyce will allow no half measures. His book is about paralysis—both the word and the thing fascinate a small boy on the first page—and paralysis is uncompromisingly asserted as something to make the flesh creep. Each one of the stories cries out against the frustration and squalor of the priest-ridden, pub-besotted, culturally decomposing urban lower-middle-class living it depicts. An elderly priest dies in a state of mental and perhaps moral degeneration, and a child to whom he has given some instruction learns from whispering women that the trouble began when he dropped and broke a chalice. Two boys play truant and have a casual encounter with an ineffective pervert. A coarse amorist, to the admiration of a less accomplished friend, gets money out of a servant girl. A drunken clerk is scolded by a bullying employer and humiliated in a public house; he goes home and flogs his son. In another public house a traveller in tea falls down the steps of a lavatory and injures himself. While convalescent he is visited by friends, who talk tediously and ignorantly about ecclesiastical matters, and then endeavour to reform him by taking him to hear a sermon for business men. It is recorded by Joyce's brother that lavatory, bedside and church in this story are designed in a ludicrous correspondence to Dante's Inferno, Purgatorio and Paradiso.

We may well agree that the style in which such incidents as these are recounted should be 'scrupulously mean'. And a great part of their effect lies in Joyce's virtuosity here. It is largely a matter of the tact with which a mimetic or semiventriloquial technique is employed. In a story about a very simple girl we read:

One time there used to be a field there in which they used to play every evening with other people's children. Then a man from Belfast bought the field and built houses in it.

And similarly with the adults. The quality of their living is defined by the language:

One said that he had seen Mac an hour before in Westmoreland Street. At this Lenehan said that he had been with Mac the night before in Egan's. The young man who had seen Mac in Westmoreland Street asked was it true that Mac had won a bit over a billiard match. Lenehan did not know: he said that Holohan had stood them drinks in Egan's.

Even an exclamation mark may be made to do this sort of work:

> Just as they were naming their poisons who should come in but Higgens!

Higgens, thus acclaimed, is a cipher; he has not appeared before and will not appear again. Such effects would be wearisome if unrelieved; and so the texture of the prose is unobtrusively varied. The first story, that of the priest who broke the chalice, begins in a child's words of one syllable, but presently the priest has a handkerchief which is 'inefficacious', and he lies 'solemn and copious' in his coffin. Everywhere the description and evocation have a precision and economy and sensitiveness which constitute the reality of the book's style just as the 'scrupulous meanness' constitutes its appearance. The style is in fact ironic, contriving to expose what it affects to accept.

A striking use of this technique occurs at the end of 'Ivy Day in the Committee Room'. We are introduced to a group of canvassers in a Dublin municipal election. They are working only for the money they hope to get from their candidate, whom they despise and distrust and would be quite ready to desert. This, with much more of the degradation of civic and national life which they represent, emerges through the medium of conversation which eventually turns on Charles Parnell, the leader of the Irish nationalist movement, who had died shortly after being driven out of political life by opponents who had exploited his involvement in a divorce case. One of those present is persuaded to recite an appropriate poem of his own composition. It begins:

> He is dead. Our Uncrowned King is dead.
>   O, Erin, mourn with grief and woe
> For he lies dead whom the fell gang
>   Of modern hypocrites laid low.

The verses, which continue in a vein of facile patriotic sentiment and factitious indignation against the treachery that had brought Parnell to ruin, read as if they might have been picked out of a forgotten popular newspaper, but they are a clever fabrication by Joyce himself. And the effect achieved is subtle. The poem is fustian; and its massed clichés and threadbare poeticisms declare it to belong to the same world of impoverished feeling conveyed in the preceding conversations. But that is not quite all. There is a ghost in the poem, the ghost of generous enthusiasms and of strong and sincere attachments to large impersonal purposes. We respond both ways, as we are later to do to analogous outcrops of romantic clichés in the reveries of Dedalus.

It is in the last and longest story in *Dubliners*, 'The Dead', that Joyce's stature as a writer first declares itself unmistakably. Two old ladies and their niece, all obscure figures in the musical life of Dublin, are giving their annual party, and to this their nephew Gabriel Conroy, a schoolmaster with literary tastes, brings his wife Gretta. The party, which is an undistinguished, rather vulgar but entirely human affair, is described with a particularity in which the influence of Flaubert may be supposed. Gabriel takes prescriptively a leading part, although his superior education and his sensitiveness prevent his doing it easily, and he makes a speech which we are given in full. This speech, like the poem in 'Ivy Day in the Committee Room', is an example of Joyce's deftest double-talk. It is full of trite and exaggerated sentiment, dwelling on spacious days gone beyond recall, absent faces, memories the world will not willingly let die, and so forth; and Gabriel is himself aware of its insincerity as he speaks. But we ourselves are correspondingly aware that it represents a kindly attempt to perform a duty and give innocent pleasure; and our attitude to Gabriel remains sympathetic even while we are being afforded a searching view of him. After the party he and his wife drive through the snow to the hotel where they are to spend the night. He is full of desire for her, but she does not respond, and presently he learns that a song heard at the party has reminded her of a boy, Michael Furey, of whom he has never heard, and who died long ago as the result of a passionate vigil he had kept for Gretta when he was already very ill. Gabriel's realization that he has been a stranger to what is thus revealed as the deepest experience of his wife's life now becomes the deepest experience of his:

A shameful consciousness of his own person assailed him. He saw himself as a ludicrous figure, acting as a pennyboy for his aunts, a nervous, well-meaning sentimentalist, orating to vulgarians and idealizing his own clownish lusts. . . .

Generous tears filled Gabriel's eyes. He had never felt like that himself towards any woman, but he knew that such a feeling must be love. The tears gathered more thickly in his eyes and in the partial darkness he imagined he saw the form of a young man standing under a dripping tree. Other forms were near. His soul had approached that region where dwell the vast hosts of the dead. He was conscious of, but could not apprehend, their wayward and flickering existence. His own identity was fading out into a grey impalpable world: the solid world itself, which these dead had one time reared and lived in, was dissolving and dwindling.

A few light taps upon the pane made him turn to the window. It had begun to snow again. He watched sleepily the flakes, silver and dark, falling obliquely against the lamplight. . . . Yes, the newspapers were right: snow was general all over Ireland. It was falling on every part of the dark central plain, on the treeless hills, falling softly upon the Bog of Allen and, farther westward, softly falling into the dark mutinous Shannon waves. It was falling, too, upon every part of the lonely churchyard on the hill where Michael Furey lay buried. It lay thickly drifted on the crooked crosses and headstones, on the spears of the little gate, on the barren thorns. His soul swooned slowly as he heard the snow falling faintly through the universe and faintly falling, like the descent of their last end, upon all the living and the dead.

'The Dead' mingles naturalism and symbolism with a new confidence and richness; tragic ironies play across it subtly and economically; its parts are proportioned to each other strangely but with brilliant effectiveness. And if its artistry looks forward to a great deal in Joyce's subsequent writings, its charity and sympathy are qualities to which he was never to allow so free a play again.

V

A Portrait of the Artist as a Young Man, essentially the story of Joyce's own break with the Catholic Church and discovery of his true vocation, was published in 1916, at the end of a process of gestation covering many years. Joyce had begun an autobiographical novel while still in his teens, and he persevered with it until it was 150,000 words long and could be regarded as approximately half finished. About 1908 he decided to rewrite the book on a smaller scale and different method, and it appears probable that the greater part of the original manuscript was then destroyed. The only considerable fragment certainly preserved, which has been published under Joyce's original title of *Stephen Hero*, is rather longer than the whole perfected work but corresponds only to the final third of it. The technique of *Stephen Hero* is objective, explicit and ploddingly documentary. It is the only one of Joyce's works self-evidently and at once to rebut Wyndham Lewis's charge that here is a writer stimulated only by ways of doing things, and not by things to be done. It thus has some claim to be considered as a substantive work, with an illuminating place in the development of Joyce's writing, and it certainly possesses the curious interest of closely defining the whole basic structure of Joyce's personality. Nevertheless the mature *Portrait* is of altogether superior artistic significance. Its opening sentence exhibits the new technique:

ONCE upon a time and a very good time it was there was a moocow coming down along the road and this moocow that was coming down along the road met a nicens little boy named baby tuckoo.

Our knowledge of Stephen is now going to come to us meditated through his own developing consciousness. That consciousness is to be the theatre of whatever drama the book attempts to present, and at the same time a territory sufficiently broad for the exercise of the vigorous naturalism which Joyce has been learning from continental masters. Yet with a quite bare naturalism he is no longer to be content, and on the second page we come upon him putting unobtrusively into operation a different sort of machinery:

The Vances lived in number seven. They had a different father and mother. They were Eileen's father and mother. When they were grown up he was going to marry Eileen. He hid under the table. His mother said:—O, Stephen will apologise.
Dante said:
—O, if not, the eagles will come and pull out his eyes.—

> Pull out his eyes,
> Apologise,
> Apologise,
> Pull out his eyes.

The whole *Portrait* is an apologia: at the same time its cardinal assertion is that Stephen will *not* apologize; rather he awaits the eagles. Joyce's eyes, moreover, were in actual fact threatened from the first; presently in the *Portrait* Stephen as a schoolboy is going to be unjustly punished as a consequence of defective vision; the master who beats him has just declared twice over that a boy's guilt may be seen in his eye; the complex of ideas thus established remains with Stephen and is several times resumed in *Ulysses*—in a manner fully intelligible only to a reader equipped with the relevant memories of the *Portrait*. This technique of weaving elusive symbolic themes percurrently through the strongly realistic fabric of his writing is something that Joyce is to exploit more and more. His prose at length becomes a vast hall of echoes—and one fatally adapted (the toiling inquirer must feel) to the conflicting voices of scholiasts. Eventually Joyce appears to have enjoyed playing up to his commentators. 'Eins within a space', we read in *Finnegans Wake*, 'and a wearywide space it wast, ere wohned a Mookse.' The relationship of the mookse to the moocow opens a wide field for conjecture.

The development of young men destined to be artists was already in Britain, as on the Continent, a prolific field of fiction, but this scarcely qualifies the large originality of the *Portrait*, which is as much a landmark in the English novel as is *Joseph Andrews* or *Middlemarch* or *The Way of All Flesh*. We have only to think of that novel's line of representative young men—Roderick Random, Tom Jones, David Copperfield, Arthur Pendennis, Richard Feverel—to realize that Stephen Dedalus is presented to us with a hitherto unexampled intimacy and immediacy. It is true that this is achieved at some cost to the vitality of the book as a whole. Here, as later in parts of *Ulysses*, we are locked up firmly inside Stephen's head; and there are times when we feel like shouting to be let out. What Stephen takes for granted, we have to take for granted too; and as he is aware of other people only as they affect his own interior chemistry, there is often something rather shadowy about the remaining personages in the book. But the picture is always clear and hard in its exhibition of Stephen's successive predicaments. The imaginative and unathletic small boy, hard pressed by the narrow orthodoxies and hovering brutalities of a Jesuit boarding school; his growing realization of his family's drift into squalor, and the pride and arrogance which he progressively summons to his aid; the overwhelming sense of sin into which the severity of Catholic doctrine precipitates him upon the occasion of his untimely sexual initiation; the breaking of his nerve and his phase of anxious and elaborate religious observance; his stumbling but implacable advance, through reverie and through conversation with whatever acquaintances will listen, upon an understanding of the realm of art and his elected place in it; the crisis of his break with Church and family, and the exalting moment of revelation and dedication on the strand: all these are vividly realized and rendered experiences.

In the *Portrait* Joyce abandons that aggressively frugal and monotonous prose, pervasive in *Stephen Hero*, out of which he had evolved the highly expressive 'scrupulous meanness' of *Dubliners*. Vocabulary, syntax, rhythm are now boldly varied to accentuate the contours of the underlying emotion, and Joyce is thus beginning to deploy his resources as a master of imitative form. *Ulysses*, considered in point of prose style, is to reveal itself quite frankly as a museum displaying, as in a series of show-cases, all the old ways of using English and a great many new ones as well. The *Portrait*, although in some degree looking forward to this, renders an overriding impression of unity, since each of the styles reflects one facet of Stephen, who is a highly unified creation. 'He chronicled with patience what he saw', we are told, 'detaching himself from it and tasting its mortifying flavour in secret.' This Stephen is best represented in some of the conversations—which, as in *Dubliners*, are based upon an ear and intellect so alert as to combine a maximum of significant statement with a minimum of apparent selection. The early scene in which Stephen's father and Mrs Riordan quarrel over Irish politics during dinner on Christmas day is Joyce's early masterpiece in this kind. When Stephen ceases to be merely a recording intelligence, and responds actively to the challenge of a world he finds so largely inimical, the style reaches out at once for weapons and armour, its whole tone becoming an extension of Stephen's most caustic and arrogant condemnations; of Dublin which has 'shrunk with time to a faint mortal odour', of Ireland 'the old sow that eats her farrow', of her church which is 'the scullery-maid of christendom'. Stephen himself is 'a priest of the eternal imagination', and he speaks in cold exalted phrases consonant with the role.

But there is yet another Stephen in the book, the Stephen who ceaselessly communes with himself on solitary walks about Dublin. It is here—it is in the style Joyce largely

employs in rendering Stephen *chez lui*—that the success of
the *Portrait* trembles in the balance. The hazard is not the
consequence of any simple miscalculation of effect; it is a
necessary risk involved in the complexity of what Joyce
attempts. There are always two lights at play on Stephen.
In the one he is seen as veritably possessing the sanctity and
strength he claims—for he has been set aside, not of his own
will, to serve the highest. In the other he is only the eldest
of Simon Dedalus's neglected children, and his aspirations
have the pathos he is to discern in his sister Dilly, when
she shyly produces the tattered French grammar she has
bought from a stall. Moreover, he is an adolescent as well
as an artist; and the emotions of adolescence are often both
disturbingly self-indulgent and much in excess of their
specific precipitating occasions—expressing themselves in
maudlin tags, conventional postures, phrases and cadences
caught up out of books, sometimes hovering agonizingly
between sublimity and absurdity, histeria and inspiration.
It is because of all this that Stephen is represented as out-
rageously sentimentalizing himself and regularly clothing
his poignantly felt nakedness in the faded splendours of a
bygone poetic rhetoric:

He heard the choir of voices in the kitchen echoed and multiplied
through an endless reverberation of the choirs of endless generations
of children and heard in all the echoes an echo also of the recurring note
of weariness and pain. All seemed weary of life even before entering
upon it. And he remembered that Newman had heard this note also in
the broken lines of Virgil, *giving utterance, like the voice of Nature herself,
to that pain and weariness yet hope of better things which has been the experience
of her children in every time.*

In this kind of writing the key is regularly pitched not to
the objective scale of its occasion, but to the dimensions of
that occasion as they exist at the moment for the boy. Thus
Stephen takes part in some theatricals in the presence of the
girl he admires, and the situation excites and disturbs him.
So we have:

He hardly knew where he was walking. Pride and hope and desire like crushed herbs in his heart sent up vapours of maddening incense before the eyes of his mind. He strode down the hill amid the tumult of sudden risen vapours of wounded pride and fallen hope and baffled desire. They streamed upwards before his anguished eyes in dense and maddening fumes and passed away above him till at last the air was clear and cold again.

Before places like this, or those far more highly wrought pages of the same sort which describe the boy's miserable frequenting of the brothels of the city, one of Joyce's best critics is surely wrong in speaking of 'purple passages that have faded considerably'. They remain highly expressive, like Juliet's hysteria or Hamlet's rant in Ophelia's grave.

At the book's crisis this boldly heightened writing is employed with great skill. Stephen's coming to his true vocation is by way of successive sensuous impressions each of which has a sort of trigger action upon forces which have been building themselves up in his mind. The piety which he has evinced since abandoning and repenting his carnal sins has suggested that he is apt for the priesthood, and the question of whether he has indeed a vocation is put to him temperately and wisely by a Jesuit director. His pride and arrogance are brought into play; he is tempted by the thought of secret knowledge and power. He is tempted, too, without clearly knowing it, as an artist: the 'vague acts of the priesthood' attract him 'by reason of their semblance of reality and of their distance from it'. On the threshold of the college the director gives Stephen his hand 'as if already to a companion in the spiritual life'. But Stephen feels the caress of a mild evening air, sees a group of young men walking with linked arms, hears a drift of music from a concertina. And these impressions are reinforced by memories of his schooldays:

His lungs dilated and sank as if he were inhaling a warm moist unsustaining air and he smelt again the moist warm air which hung in the bath in Clongowes above the sluggish turfcoloured water.

Some instinct, waking at these memories, stronger than education or piety, quickened within him at every near approach to that life, an instinct subtle and hostile, and armed him against acquiescence.

Yet still his mind oscillates. He is entered at the university, and celebrates the occasion with comical portentousness in an elaborately harmonious reverie. But this in turn brings to his mind 'a proud cadence from Newman'—

Whose feet are as the feet of harts and underneath the everlasting arms

—and 'the pride of that dim image brought back to his mind the dignity of the office he had refused . . . The oils of ordination would never anoint his body. He had refused.' Why? The answer—the positive answer—comes as he walks on the beach. It is, in fact, the secular artist's reply to the 'proud cadence' of Newman:

He drew forth a phrase from his treasure and spoke it softly to himself;
—A day of dappled seaborne clouds.

This is Stephen Dedalus's moment of apocalypse. He realizes that he has apprehended something beautiful. Soon he will be able to write in his diary the final truth about himself: 'I desire to press in my arms the loveliness which has not yet come into the world.' It is only a shallow irony that would remark that this loveliness is to be represented by Leopold and Molly Bloom in *Ulysses*. Nor need we contemn, in the name of sophisticated restraint, the pitch of the prose in which this moment, a moment at once of final release and final submission, is celebrated:

Where was his boyhood now? Where was the soul that had hung back from her destiny, to brood alone upon the shame of her wounds and in her house of squalor and subterfuge to queen it in faded cerements and in wreaths that withered at the touch? Or where was he?
He was alone. He was unheeded, happy and near to the wild heart of life. He was alone and young and wilful and wildhearted, alone amid

a waste of wild air and brackish waters and the sea-harvest of shells and tangle and veiled grey sunlight and gayclad lightclad figures of children and girls and voices childish and girlish in the air.

The whole hymn of praise and dedication and pride has still its aspect of precariousness and pathos; preserves, for all its gorgeousness the poignancy of the boy's cry in *Stephen Hero*: 'Mother . . . I'm young, healthy, happy. What is the crying for?' Stephen, in a last analysis, is singing only as his brothers and sisters have been singing a few pages earlier, when that could be detected in their voices which Newman had heard in the broken lines of Virgil.

VI

In the penultimate section of *Ulysses* (1922), which takes the form of a long catechism, Leopold Bloom is described in bed at the end of the day. He is curled up, we are told, like a child in the womb. And the section concludes thus:

Womb? Weary?
He rests. He has travelled.

With?

Sindbad the Sailor and Tinbad the Tailor and Jinbad the Jailer and Whinbad the Whaler and Ninbad the Nailer and Finbad the Failer and Binbad the Bailer and Pinbad the Pailer and Mindbad the Mailer and Hinbad the Hailer and Rinbad the Railer and Dinbad the Kailer. and Vinbad the Quailer and Linbad the Yailer and Xinbad the Phthailer

When?

Going to dark bed there was a square round Sinbad the Sailor roc's auk's egg in the night of the bed of all the auks of the rocs of Darkinbad the Brightdayler.

Where?

Bloom has travelled as the whole crowd of us must travel. But the final question *Where?* is unanswered and ambiguous. If we stress the All-life-in-a-day aspect of *Ulysses* it is a question about futurity, and there is no answer to it on any premises that Joyce admits. If we think simply of 16 June 1904, then Bloom's journey is from the waking world to the world of dream, and there is a sense in which *Where?* receives its answer in Joyce's next book. Bloom has fallen asleep; we have accompanied him just over the threshold and thereby gained a preliminary glimpse of the vast territory of the unconscious mind into which we are to be conducted in *Finnegans Wake*. The jingle of names (as well as making the statement 'Bloom=Everyman=Us') is hypnoidal, and the syntactical obscurity of *a square round Sinbad* and the strange resonance in *Darkinbad the Bright-dayler* expresses the violence done by the unconscious and its queer categories to the logic of waking life.

A positive response to Joyce's writing as a whole depends upon the ability to accept such uses of language as this passage adumbrates. Some readers find it endlessly fascinating. Others declare it boring, and assert Joyce to be simply one who, solemn and wide awake, adds Finbad to Ninbad till the cows come home. There can be no doubt that he became compulsively addicted to letting words fool around, and that his brain was the most elaborately equipped play-ground for the purpose that has ever left a record of itself in literature. Whether he is to be indicted of progressive artistic irresponsibility makes a hard question, not likely to be well answered either by fanatical Joyceans or by those who turn away from his books in disgust and indignation.

The action of the *Portrait* extends over many years, in a manner traditional enough in the novel. *Ulysses* is revolutionary in this regard, being a work of great length in which the entire action is organized, as in a classical play, so as to fall within a single revolution of the sun. Yet it begins precisely as if it were a continuation of the *Portrait*, with the thread taken up after the hero's brief absence from Ireland. In fact it represents a curious amalgam of just such a sequel with a wholly different project which Joyce had entertained during the period of *Dubliners*. 'Ulysses' was to have been the title of a short story descriptive of a day's wandering about Dublin on the part of a certain Mr Hunter. The ironic association of this personage with the Homeric hero was later enriched through a further association with the Wandering Jew, and from this fusion Leopold Bloom was born. Then Joyce having hit upon the notion of a loosely organized structural correspondence with the *Odyssey*, perceived that he could begin with a *Telemachia*, in which the central figure would still be Stephen Dedalus.

But the opening pages, although they have indeed an unforgettable largeness as of great painting, scarcely persuade us that we want to hear much more about Joyce's former hero. Stephen has not been improved by his residence in France. Indeed, we are already more likely to have admired the art of the *Portrait* than the personality of its protagonist. And although that criticism is obviously defective which depreciates the book on the score that Stephen is a prig or a cold fish, it yet remains true that part of a novelist's material, however austere a realist he be, consists in the sympathy of his reader; that he must learn to manipulate this like everything else; and that to miscalculate here is to invite disaster. In *Ulysses* Stephen is more insufferable than his creator appears disposed to admit. His weariness, his hauteur, his curiously hinted proneness to indulge a dream life in the University of Oxford, his disposition to speak 'quietly', 'coldly', 'bitterly' ('It is a symbol of Irish art. The cracked looking-glass of a servant'), even his dislike of water and presumably of soap: all these are facets of his character that invite fairly enough the jibes of Wyndham Lewis. When presently Stephen is discovered teaching school we find ourselves disposed to question his declared unfitness for the task, since his mental habit is represented as almost wholly pedantic. This impression is intensified in the succeeding section, which presents us with Stephen's highly allusive and recondite stream of consciousness as he walks on the strand, and which begins thus:

> Ineluctable modality of the visible: at least that if no more, thought through my eyes. Signatures of all things I am here to read, seaspawn and seawrack, the nearing tide, that rusty boot. Snotgreen, bluesilver, rust: coloured signs. Limits of the diaphane. But he adds: in bodies. Then he was aware of them bodies before of them coloured. How? By knocking his sconce against them, sure. Go easy. Bald he was and a millionaire, *maestro di color che sanno*. Limit of the diaphane in. Why in? Diaphane, adiaphane.

Part of the obscurity results from Joyce's demand that our consciousness should be steadily at play over the entire surface of his work, so that phrases and associations are intelligible only in the light of others scores or hundreds of pages away. This is a legitimate device, and the extent of its use is a matter of literary tact: the more serious the under-taking, the more vigorous the co-operation we may fairly be expected to bring to it. But so much in Stephen's reverie is resistant to any ready elucidation that we come to wonder whether all this showing off to himself (if that is it) might have been more succinctly accomplished had his creator been less concerned to show off to us.

Certainly Stephen is a Telemachus to whom Ulysses, in the figure of Bloom, comes decidedly to the rescue, so far as the general artistic success of the book is concerned. Whether, within the fable, Bloom ultimately means much to Stephen, or Stephen to Bloom, is a question which has been variously answered by critics. Considered as an action, *Ulysses* ends in obscurity, whether inadvertent or deliberate. But considered as a theatre of novel design, constructed in the main for the exhibition of a comic character of striking vitality and verisimilitude, it is an unchallengeable even if dauntingly laboured success.

For Lewis, once more—always the best *advocatus diaboli* when we are judging Joyce—Bloom is a walking cliché;

beneath a vast technical elaborateness in the presentation is an orthodox comic figure of the simplest outline. It is certainly true that the lifelikeness of Bloom does not proceed from his being very directly observed from the life. He is a highly evolved literary creation, and his complexity—for he is complex—is literary. Some aspects of him exist only because a body of Anglo-Irish humour existed; others, only because *Bouvard et Pécuchet* existed. But his principal derivation is surely from the mock-heroic tradition. It has been asserted on eminent authority that the *Odyssey* provided Joyce merely with a scaffolding which a reader may disregard. This is not so. To anyone who has got the hang of the book, Ὀδυσσεὺς πολύτροπος, the much-travelled Ulysses, is sufficiently present to make Bloom seem absurd and diminutive. Yet, as with the best mock-heroic, the reference is capable too of working the other way. Bloom's positive qualities, his representative character, his pathos, all take point from his original.

An elaborate and considered craft is evident too in the medium in which Bloom is presented to us. Joyce had found Edouard Dujardin's *Les Lauriers sont coupés*, a short novel published in 1887, a technique of internal monologue which in *Ulysses* he develops with immense resource and cunning. Once more he is far from drawing directly on life. Bloom never stops talking to himself—except just occasionally when he talks to someone else—and we are bound to feel that this assiduity in verbalization, although convenient both to his creator and to us who would make his acquaintance, is something quite outside nature. Yet Joyce achieves with it a vivid and deep illusion. The content of Bloom's mind, his interests, his responses to stimuli, are depicted with deliberation as very much those of any vulgar, curious, kindly man. To give just that with unexampled fullness is largely the idea of the book, and it carries with it the danger of a rather boring lack of particularity. Yet we become convinced that Bloom's mind is not quite like any other mind. It is indeed with his mind as with his hat. On 16 June

1904, many Dubliners must have been wearing a high-grade
hat from Plasto's, but only Bloom can have been wearing a
high-grade ha. We suspect a misprint (as we often do) but
are in the presence of a device. Bloom's internal idiom, too,
is consistently and not too obtrusively idiosyncratic. A
traditional literary resource—one exploited alike by the
creators of Hamlet and Mr Jingle—has been deftly trans-
ferred to a new theatre.

Bloom admits us more generously to his intimacy than
does almost any other figure in fiction. Yet he is a small
man; neither nature nor nurture has given him much; his
moral being, which is amoebic, and his intellectual interests,
which if lively are circumscribed, prove alike unreward-
ing to exploration on the scale proposed by the book. Bloom
thus comes, for all his liveliness and attractiveness, to shoot
his bolt with us just as Stephen has done. His environment
threatens to swamp him; he ceases to float upon the current
of his creator's abounding imaginative vitality and is felt
as battling rather desperately against it. It is perhaps by way
of redressing a balance here that Joyce offers us finally,
and so much at large, the figure of Molly Bloom, the sadly
faithless Penelope of the story.

Mrs Bloom is essentially passive. In the morning she
accepts breakfast in bed from the hands of her husband; in
the afternoon, again in bed, she entertains the irresistible
Blazes Boylan; in the small hours, in bed still, she indulges
herself in the enormous reverie with which the book concludes. The sustained erotic tension of this, which takes about
two hours to read, reflects more credit upon Joyce than upon
Mr Boylan. Totally without punctuation (although, for
some reason, divided into eight enormous paragraphs), it
appears concerned to carry the technique of internal monologue to something near its theoretical limit. And it does
achieve, for all its psychological implausibility, an exhibition as of some vast sprawled and monolithic image of
female sexuality. Bloom, on the other hand, is throughout
in restless motion; he visits the pork butcher, feeds the cat,

attends a funeral, pursues his profession as an advertisement tout, has a row in a pub, misconducts himself on a beach, and so on. His most characteristic motion is a wriggle—through inhospitable doors and past averted shoulders. He remains symbolically, if not very impressively, male.

If the Blooms have anything in common it is a retrospective turn of mind. Characters or events in *Dubliners* frequently recur to them. Bloom, engaged on one of his morning duties, recalls how, long ago, he used to jot down on his cuff what his wife said when dressing. 'What had Gretta Conroy on?' she had once asked. Bartell d'Arcy, whose singing of *The Lass of Aughrim* called up for Gretta the shade of Michael Furey, has been among Mrs Bloom's lovers; and so has Lenehan, once the admirer of that Corley who wheedled the gold coin from a servant-girl. Mrs. Bloom during her vigil recalls, among numerous other prominent citizens, 'Tom Kernan that drunken little barrelly man that bit his tongue off falling down the men's WC drunk in some place or other'. Two of the friends who took Kernan to a retreat for business men join Bloom at the funeral at Glasnevin; and Bloom reflects that his last visit there was for the funeral of Mrs Sinico—of whose unfortunate end we have read in a short story called 'A Painful Case', Simon Dedalus—another of Mrs Bloom's bedfellows, is perhaps a little changed, even as his family is further degraded; in some regards an engaging character, he now speaks with a violent foulness and out of a deep venom absent from the *Portrait*. All this reminiscence reflects Joyce's own mind, which we feel to repose in the Dublin of his youth in a quite extraordinary way. He is nowhere able, or at least disposed, to set out for the past as upon an act of exploration. He has carried the past along with him in his consciousness—as he carried, it is said, its newspapers and tram-tickets along with him in his trunks. It is not indeed wholly true that, as Lewis avers, his thought was 'of a conventional and fixed order' which remained unchanged since his early days. *Ulysses* differs from the *Portrait* not merely in elaboration, display, technical variousness and virtuosity. It mirrors deeper responses to the whole spectacle of enjoying and suffering humanity. But the spectacle itself is confined to the same stage; the old props are trundled on and off; and we are progressively aware of an inflexibly willed, rather desperate resourcefulness as the sustaining principle of the whole. And the resourcefulness is—surely to a hazardous degree—linguistic and stylistic. *Ulysses* is quite staggeringly full of language. The stuff comes at us in great rollers, breakers, eddies and tumbles of spume and spray. It is wildly exhilarating. It is also rather buffeting, bruising, exhausting long before the end.

There is evidence that Joyce gave anxious and sustained thought to the form and structure of his work. He certainly let his disciples suppose so; they are fond of expounding the successive episodes in terms of an intricate superimposition of framework upon framework: organs, arts, colours, symbols and technics. Read however without all this instruction, *Ulysses* may strike us as a large-scale improvisation, a hand-to-mouth progression from stunt to stunt—with nearly all the stunts coming quite brilliantly off—but to a final effect of agglomeration before which any summing up, any secure arriving at a right aesthetic total, is singularly hard to achieve.

A curious encyclopaedism, such as may be found in certain medieval poets, obsesses the author of *Ulysses*. He seems to feel, for instance, that his book should contain not only his own sort of English—or rather his own sorts of English in their almost inexhaustible variety—but every other sort of English as well; and so he writes one long section, that in which Bloom visits the National Maternity Hospital in Holles Street and meets Stephen, in a succession of parodies tracing the whole evolution of English prose. Some of these are presented out of order; and we are told by the commentators that as this evolution of styles is being appropriately exhibited in a context of development from unfertilized ovum to birth, and as, in an embryo, one or another organ may in fact develop prematurely, there is a particular grace in setting the parodies too in an occasional chronological confusion. Joyce's mind, we must recognize, is as tortuous and pedantic as it is prodigal and—in essentials—poetic. And its prodigality seems to render very uncertain its sense of measure. Between the longest section of the book, the unparalleled and astounding fantasia of the unconscious, thronged and farced with spectres of preternatural vigour and overpowering horror, which opens at 'the Mabbot street entrance of nighttown'—between this, and the contrasting but equally unexampled long slow earthen pulse of Mrs Bloom's concluding reverie, there is obviously required some episode of relaxed tension. Joyce provides two such episodes in succession. First, Bloom and Stephen are to be represented as sitting in a cabmen's shelter, exhausted. This exhaustion is to be conveyed, on the governing principle of the book, by recourse to an exhausted, a jejune prose. Joyce therefore contrives what is best described as a sustained cliché of some twenty thousand words. Next the two men—casually thrown together but symbolically regarded as profoundly in search of each other—make their way to Bloom's kitchen. They are isolated individuals, souls struggling towards some obscure self-realization through and against the recalcitrant medium of matter. This recalcitrant medium Joyce evokes overwhelmingly by a yet longer and denser device: an interminable inexorable catechism, couched almost exclusively in a flat scientific jargon, exhaustively tabulating not only Bloom's present physical environment but also that of the dream-cottage to which he aspires to retire:

What homothetic objects, other than the candlestick, stood on the mantelpiece?

A timepiece of striated Connemara marble, stopped at the hour of 4.46 a.m. on the 21 March 1896, matrimonial gift of Matthew Dillon: a dwarf tree of glacial arborescence under a transparent bellshade, matrimonial gift of Luke and Caroline Doyle: an embalmed owl, matrimonial gift of Alderman John Hooper.

There are more than three hundred such answers to questions, and some of them describe with minute particularity as many as ten or twenty separate objects. Joyce is said to have taken more pride in this part of *Ulysses* than in any other. Certainly it cannot be called idle or even—strangely enough—boring, and there is no reason to suppose that the precise effect it produces could be produced in any other way. Yet this massive accumulation, this enormous *stasis*, is presented to us at a point where we suppose ourselves to be moving towards the resolution of a fable. What, we ask is this resolution? The mountain has laboured. But where is the mouse?

Stripped and viewed as an action, *Ulysses* reveals itself as being much what it started out to be: a short story in *Dubliners*. We need not suppose that Mr Hunter's wanderings about Dublin were to have been no more than a small exercise in the picaresque. That was never Joyce's way. Something always happens in his stories—but it is generally a small, muted, problematically or evanescently significant thing. Most characteristically, it is an encounter—an encounter with some circumscribed hinted consequence which is not pursued. And this is the formula of *Ulysses*, the spare skeleton which has been given so much flesh and so many clothes. None of the great elaborative works of literature—Milton's *Paradise Lost*, Goethe's *Faust*, Mann's *Joseph und seine Brüder*—has made do with quite so little.

Yet this strange book—so *voulu*, so wilfully tedious, so dirty, often smelling so queerly of pedagogy and examination papers—is one to which mature readers will return again and again. We revisit it—Mr Edmund Wilson has excellently said—as we revisit a city, a city animated by a complex inexhaustible life. Its material may be 'consciously the decay of a mournful province'—the words are Lewis's once more—but it is not itself mournful. And it is not negative. It closes, with passion, on a basic affirmation: 'yes I said yes I will Yes.'

VII

Ulysses, the record of a single day, exhausts the exploration
of the waking mind. *Finnegans Wake*, the formidable work
to the elaborating of which Joyce devoted the last fifteen
years of his life, is correspondingly the record of a single
night; and it proposes to interpret, with an equal exhaustive-
ness, the nature and content of the mind asleep. To this
tremendous proposal Joyce was in part driven by the logic
of his own achievement, in part encouraged by the drift of
contemporary psychological speculation, and in part lured
by the unparalleled opportunities which the fabricating of
a dream language would afford to his remarkable logopoeic
faculty.

As if conscious that he had revealed no genius for that
sort of large-scale fiction which has significantly a beginning, a middle and an end, Joyce framed this final work
upon a peculiar principle. It begins:

riverrun, past Eve and Adam's, from swerve of shore to bend of bay,
brings us by a commodius vicus of recirculation back to Howth Castle
and Environs.

And it ends:

A way a lone a last a loved a long the

The last sentence in fact runs straight into the first. Ideally,
the text should be disposed not in a bound volume but in a
single line of type round an enormous wheel. History,
Joyce now believed, is such a wheel, and its revolution has
been explained by the eighteenth-century Italian philo-
sopher, Giambattista Vico. The 'commodius vicus of recirculation' introduces us to Vico and his theory as well as
to a pleasant *giro* that may be taken round Dublin bay.
Howth Castle and Environs display initial letters preluding
the entry of the book's central character, Humphrey

Chimpden Earwicker. But as Earwicker is a universal figure, the initials may also stand for Haveth Childers Everywhere or Here Comes Everybody. Eve and Adam's is the popular name for a church on the bank of the Liffey, which is the river that is running in the opening word; but as we are already talking about the stream of history, we are no doubt being invited, incidentally, to consider that stream's first welling-up in the Garden of Eden.

Joyce is said to have declared in a moment of arrogance (which may indeed have been softened by humour) that the demand he made upon his reader was no less than the application of a lifetime. Certainly he now had little regard for anything that can be approximated to lucidity, a fact which becomes apparent as soon as we go on from the first paragraph to the second:

> Sir Tristram, violer d'amores, fr'over the short sea, had passencore rearrived from North Armorica on this side the scraggy isthmus of Europe Minor to wielderfight his penisolate war: nor had topsawyer's rocks by the stream Oconee exaggerated themselse to Laurens County's gorgios while they went doublin their mumper all the time: nor avoice frou afire bellowsed mishe mishe to tauftauf thuartpeatrick: not yet, though venissoon after, had a kidscad buttended a bland old isaac: not yet, though all's fair in vanessy, were sosie sesthers wroth with twone nathandjoe. Rot a peck of pa's malt had Jhem or Shen brewed by arclight and rory end to the regginbrow was to be seen ringsome on the aquaface.

'The first impression', Mr Campbell and Mr Robinson say of this in the volume which they have devoted to a preliminary exegesis of *Finnegans Wake*, 'is one of chaos, unrelieved by any landmark of meaning or recognition.' But this impression they assert to be totally mistaken, since the passage holds nothing that need shake our faith in Joyce 'as a wielder of the most disciplined logic known to modern letters'. It is surely abundantly clear, however, that as long as we assert the traditional canons of what constitutes discourse Joyce *is* producing nonsense. The passage is logical—

or claims to be logical—only in the very special sense in which (according to certain psychological theories) the most phantasmagoric dream must be logical; in the sense, that is to say, that its constituting elements are chosen and concatenated not fortuitously but as the designed product of unconscious mental processes in which may be detected the working of intelligible laws. When eventually we discover that Earwicker has a wife and daughter, and that he has reached a phase of sexual involution in which his relations with them are ambiguous, we realize the appropriateness with which the dream-logic calls up both Tristram, who had two Iseults, and Swift (*nathandjoe* being an anagram for *Jonathan*), who had Stella and Vanessa. If we ask why Vanessa is disguised as *in vanessy* we may find ourselves thinking of *Inverness* and so recalling Macbeth, who like Earwicker fell into some moral danger as a consequence of his relations with females.

It will be evident that *Finnegans Wake* offers much scope to the interpreter. The reader's first endeavour, however, should be less with the larger significances which the book is conjectured to embody than with the linguistic technique which it indubitably employs. If one considers, still in the above passage, the phrase *penisolate war* one quickly sees that it is simply *Peninsular War* (the title commonly given by historians to the Napoleonic campaigns in Spain) so distorted as to carry more secondary suggestions than one. For example, if hyphenated as *pen-isolate war* it may call up a whole complex of thoughts about Joyce himself, who certainly fought with a pen—and did so from the isolation of Trieste or Zürich. It was maintained by Freud and his followers that language regularly takes on this ambiguous character—whether in wit, or in slips of the tongue or pen—under pressure of conflicting unconscious forces. Psychoanalytic literature, moreover, reports many instances of such obscurely significant disguisings and telescopings of words being remembered from dreams; and it is evident that from this Joyce derived the notion that it should be possible to excavate—or if not to excavate to invent—a whole dream-language of this sort.

It is certain that *Finnegans Wake* is not, in any simple sense, the product of a psychic automatism. Joyce wrote much of it in comparatively plain language, which he then with great labour elaborated until he had achieved his complex final product. Of some sections of the work early and intermediate versions have been published, and at least some of these have been judged by many readers to be more successful than the later versions evolved from them. Once again we have to question Joyce's sense of measure; he overdoes it, and the eventual effect is of something mechanical or synthetic. But the mere fact that he worked over his text again and again is irrelevant in judging its merits as an artistic evocation of the world of dreams. The more one reads the book, the more is one disposed to acknowledge in it an authentic imaginative correspondence with what we know of unconscious mental life.

But *Finnegans Wake* remains a very hard book. Joyce does nothing to help us. It is only in the penultimate section that we gain anything but the most obscure and fragmentary intimations of what, in any common sense, it is all about. Moreover, to the obscurities of one psychological system Joyce has cheerfully added the obscurities of another. Earwicker, the Dublin publican, dreams obediently on Freud's principles—but when he dreams deeply enough he dreams on Jung's as well, so that his dream becomes anybody's or everybody's dream; universal knowledge, fragmented and distorted, drifts in and out after a fashion that none of the Earwicker family could conceivably compass: and we are presumably being invited to believe that we have penetrated to something like a Great Memory, or collective unconsciousness of the race. Such an exploration must almost necessarily, one supposes, be attended by a large obscurity. But it is sometimes possible to feel that we are in the presence of something much more circumscribed, and that the reduplication of darknesses in *Finnegans Wake* represents simply veil upon veil which Joyce has spun round some personal predicament, some obliquity of the private or domestic life, such as had always haunted his writing, and which he is now at the last unwilling to exhibit directly either to others or to himself.

Finnegans Wake, then, if enigmatic at a first entrance, is yet largely susceptible of elucidation both as a cunningly contrived and disposed phantasmagoria of near-dreamlike material and as an inexhaustibly subtle, even if at times depressingly dogged, campaign upon the farthest boundaries of language. What is most accessible in it is its often hauntingly beautiful melody, which is perhaps best illustrated by the famous ending of the section originally published under the title 'Anna Livia Plurabelle'. Anna Livia is the Liffey, and the Liffey is the symbol of the feminine, just as is the Hill of Howth ('Howth Castle and Environs') of the masculine. Here two washerwomen—who as well as being washerwomen are a stone and an elm, death and life—are gossiping about Anna in the gathering dusk. And their gossip—to quote Mr Edmund Wilson again—'is the voice of the river itself, light, rapid, incessant, almost metrical, now monotonously running on one note, now impeded and syncopated, but vivaciously, interminably babbling its indistinct rigmarole story, half-unearthly, half-vulgarly human, of a heroine half-legendary, half-real':

And ho! Hey? What all men. Hot? His tittering daughters of. Whawk?

Can't hear with the waters of. The chittering waters of. Flittering bats, fieldmice bawk talk. Ho! Are you not gone ahome? What Tom Malone? Can't hear with bawk of bats, all the liffeying waters of. Ho, talk save us! My foos won't moos. I feel as old as yonder elm. A tale told of Shaun or Shem? All Livia's daughtersons. Dark hawks hear us. Night! Night! My ho head halls. I feel as heavy as yonder stone. Tell me of John or Shaun? Who were Shem and Shaun the living sons or daughters of? Night now! Tell me, tell me, tell me, elm! Night night! Telmetale of stem or stone. Beside the rivering waters of, hitherandthithering waters of. Night!

Yet many who have turned to the whole work with excitement after hearing Joyce's own recorded reading of this must have been baffled and disappointed by the indigestible matter they found there. It will never conduce to Joyce's reputation to assert that *Finnegans Wake* is, in any ordinary sense, a readable book. It is not; it is in the main a closed book even to most persons of substantial literary cultivation. But if not readable it may yet be seminal; and it seems possible that, for many generations, its frequentation by a small body of writers and students will indirectly enrich the subsequent stream of English literature.

JAMES JOYCE

A Select Bibliography

(Books published in London, unless stated otherwise)

Bibliography:

JAMES JOYCE: A Bibliography of His Writings, Critical Material and Miscellanea, by Alan Parker; Boston, Mass. (1948).

'James Joyce: Addenda to Alan Parker's Bibliography', by William White, Bibliographical Society of America, *Papers*, xliii; New York (1949)
—substantially augments Parker's listing of 'critical material'; further additions are given by William White under the same title in two articles in the *James Joyce Review*, Vol. I, i and iii (June and September 1957).

A BIBLIOGRAPHY OF JAMES JOYCE (1882–1941), by John J. Slocum and Herbert Cahoon (1953)
—the standard bibliography; gives a complete account of all publications of Joyce's works up to 1950.

'Supplement to James Joyce Bibliography, 1954–1957', by Richard M. Kain, *James Joyce Review*, Vol. I, iv (December 1957).

'Further Supplement to Joyce Bibliography, 1950–1957', by A. M. Cohn, *James Joyce Review*, Vol. II, i–ii (1958).

'Further Supplemental J. J. Checklists', by A. M. Cohn are appearing annually in the *James Joyce Quarterly*.

THE PERSONAL LIBRARY OF JAMES JOYCE [in the Lockwood Memorial Library in the University of Buffalo]. A Descriptive Bibliography, by Thomas E. Connolly, Buffalo (*University of Buffalo Studies*, Vol. XXII, i, April 1955)
—records some marginalia and evidence of use.

THE CORNELL JOYCE COLLECTION: A Catalogue, by Robert Scholes; Cornell (1961).

JAMES JOYCE'S MANUSCRIPTS AND LETTERS AT THE UNIVERSITY OF BUFFALO: A Catalogue, by Peter Spielberg; Buffalo (1962).

A FIRST DRAFT VERSION OF 'FINNEGANS WAKE', ed. David Hayman (1963)
—includes a catalogue of the *Finnegans Wake* MSS in the British Museum.
Note: In addition to the collections detailed in the books listed above there is a large collection of Joyce MSS at Yale; and the original MSS of *A Portrait of the Artist* and *Ulysees* are in the National Library of Ireland and the Rosenbach Institute, respectively.

A BIBLIOGRAPHY OF JAMES JOYCE STUDIES, by Robert H. Deming; Kansas (1964)
—an annotated list of critical material on Joyce complete up to December 1961.

Selected Works:

INTRODUCING JAMES JOYCE, a selection from Joyce's prose with an introduction by T. S. Eliot (1942)
—also published in paperback.

THE PORTABLE JAMES JOYCE, ed. Harry Levin; New York (1947)
—the English edition (1948) is entitled *The Essential James Joyce*. It contains *Dubliners*, *A Portrait of the Artist*, *Exiles*, *Collected Poems*, *The Holy Office*, *Gas from a Burner*, and selections from *Ulysses* and *Finnegans Wake*.

Separate Works published before 1941:

CHAMBER MUSIC (1907)
—with notes by William Y. Tindall; New York (1954).

DUBLINERS (1914)
—Travellers' Library edition, 1926; Guild Books edition, 1947; issued as a Penguin Book, 1956.

A PORTRAIT OF THE ARTIST AS A YOUNG MAN; New York (1916)
—first published serially in *The Egoist*, 2 February 1914–1 September 1915. Travellers' Library edition, 1930, frequently reprinted; annotated edition, with notes by J. S. Atherton, 1964. 'Definitive text' corrected from Dublin holograph, 1968.

EXILES (1918)
—reprinted (1952) with some notes by Joyce and an introduction by Padraic Colum. Published in paperback 1962.

ULYSSES; Paris (1922)
—frequently reprinted; the best text is by the Odyssey Press, Hamburg
(1939). First published serially in *The Little Review*, New York,
1918–20 and *The Egoist*, 1919, but not completed in either periodical.
Published in paperback, 1969.

POMES PENYEACH; Paris (1927), London (1933).

FINNEGANS WAKE (1939)
—from April 1924 numerous fragments of *Finnegans Wake* appeared
as from 'Work in Progress'; some as pamphlets, and some in
periodicals, notably *Transition*, Paris. See Walton Litz's 'The Making
of *Finnegans Wake*', in M. Magalaner (ed.), *A James Joyce Miscellany*,
Second Series, Carbondale, Illinois, 1959.

Posthumous Works:

STEPHEN HERO, ed. Theodore Spencer (1944)
—the surviving part of the first draft of *A Portrait of the Artist*. The
reprint of 1956 (1955 New York) contained a further fragment, and
several more short fragments appeared as 'Five More Pages of
James Joyce's *Stephen Hero*' in *A James Joyce Miscellany, Second
Series*. Also published in paperback.

THE LETTERS OF JAMES JOYCE, Vol. I, ed. Stuart Gilbert (1957), Vols II
and III, ed. R. Ellmann (1966)
—Vol. I contains about 450 letters collected by Stuart Gilbert, with
an index. Vols. II and III contain over a thousand other letters,
carefully edited and with an index in Vol. III.

THE CRITICAL WRITINGS OF JAMES JOYCE, ed. Ellsworth Mason and
Richard Ellman (1959)
—includes Joyce's early essays on 'Ibsen's New Drama', 'James
Clarence Mangan', and 'The Day of the Rabblement', book
reviews, *The Holy Office*, and *Gas from a Burner*.

SCRIBBLEDEHOBBLE, ed. Thomas E. Connolly; Evanston (1961)
—a transcript of one of Joyce's largest notebooks in the Wickser
Collection in Buffalo University Library, with photographs of
some of its pages.

DANIEL DEFOE; Buffalo (1964)
—Joyce's lecture at Trieste; Italian text with a translation and notes
by J. Prescott.

THE WORKSHOP OF DAEDALUS, ed. Robert Scholes and Richard M. Kain; Evanston, Illinois (1965)
—includes Joyce's *Epiphanies*, his Paris, Pola and Trieste notebooks, and an autobiographical essay, 'A Portrait of the Artist' written when Joyce was twenty-one.

GIACOMO JOYCE, introduction and notes by R. Ellmann (1968)
—a Joyce notebook, much of which was previously published in R. Ellmann's *James Joyce*, pp. 353–60.

Some Biographical and Critical Studies:

(i) *General*

AXEL'S CASTLE: A Study in the Imaginative Literature of 1870–1930, by Edmund Wilson (1931)
—contains an admirable chapter on Joyce.

FOR CONTINUITY, by F. R. Leavis (1933)
—contains some critical discussion of Joyce.

THE NOVEL AND THE MODERN WORLD, by David Daiches; Chicago (1939)
—contains chapters on Joyce. Revised edition 1960.

JAMES JOYCE, by Herbert Gorman (1940)
—written with Joyce's help, and contains material not reproduced elsewhere. Revised edition 1948.

THE WOUND AND THE BOW: Seven Studies in Literature, by Edmund Wilson (1942)
—contains an illuminating and well-balanced discussion of *Finnegans Wake*.

JAMES JOYCE: A Critical Introduction, by Harry Levin (1944)
—first published, Norfolk, Conn., 1941, but remains the best general introduction to Joyce's work, although the additional matter in the revised edition (1960) does not reach the same high standard.

FROM SHAKESPEARE TO JOYCE, by E. E. Stoll; New York (1944).

THE CLOWN'S GRAIL, by Wallace Fowlie (1947)
—Joyce as a symbol of the quest for art.

JAMES JOYCE: Two Decades of Criticism, ed. Seon Givens; New York (1948)
—contains a number of important essays. Augmented edition, New York, 1963.

RECOLLECTIONS OF JAMES JOYCE, by Stanislaus Joyce, translated by Ellsworth Mason; New York (1950).

JAMES JOYCE: His Way of Interpreting the Modern World, by William Y. Tindall (1950).

SILENT YEARS: An Autobiography, with Memoirs of James Joyce and Our Ireland, by J. F. Byrne; New York (1953)
—an account of Joyce as a young man by the 'Cranly' of *A Portrait*.

THREE STUDIES IN TWENTIETH CENTURY OBSCURITY, by Francis Russell (1954)
—an intelligent attack on Joyce's later works.

JAMES JOYCE AND THE CULTIC USE OF FICTION, by Kristian Smidt; Oslo (1955)
—an intelligent and interesting thesis on Joyce as the founder of his own cult.

JOYCE, THE MAN, THE WORK, THE REPUTATION, by Marvin Magalaner and Richard M. Kain; New York (1956)
—assembles and comments upon a large body of critical opinion, and contains an excellent bibliography.

DUBLIN'S JOYCE, by Hugh Kenner (1956)
—intelligent and original interpretations of Joyce's work.

A JAMES JOYCE MISCELLANY, ed. Marvin Magalaner; New York (1957)
—this small book was followed by two larger and more important collections: *A James Joyce Miscellany*, *Second Series*, Carbondale, Illinois (1959), and *A James Joyce Miscellany*, *Third Series*, Carbondale (1962). They contain a wide variety of articles, some of great value.

JOYCE AND AQUINAS, by William T. Noon, S.J., Yale (1957)
—a sympathetic analysis of Joyce's use of Aquinas, which suggests that Joyce's knowledge was mainly derived from secondary sources.

JAMES JOYCE'S WORLD, by Patricia Hutchins (1957)
—recounts a pilgrimage to visit the various places in which Joyce lived. Most of the material given in an earlier book by the same writer, *James Joyce's Dublin*, is reproduced here.

MY BROTHER'S KEEPER, by Stanislaus Joyce, ed. Richard Ellmann (1958)
—interesting for the picture it gives of Stanislaus Joyce, as well as for the information about his brother.

THE SYMPATHETIC ALIEN: Joyce and Catholicism, by J. M. Morse (1959)
—considers Joyce's use of Aquinas and other patristic writers, and suggests that Joyce was well read in their works.

A READER'S GUIDE TO JAMES JOYCE, by William Y. Tindall (1959)
—a scholarly but very readable account of all Joyce's works, placing great emphasis on his use of symbols.

JAMES JOYCE, by Richard Ellmann (1959)
—the standard biography, compiled with great thoroughness.

JOYCE AMONG THE JESUITS, by Kevin Sullivan; New York (1959)
—provides information about the background to Joyce's education.

OUR FRIEND JAMES JOYCE, by Mary and Padraic Colum (1959)
—describes meetings with Joyce, the established writer.

SHAKESPEARE AND COMPANY, by Sylvia Beach; New York (1959)
—an entertaining account of her experiences by the first publisher of *Ulysses*.

SONG IN THE WORKS OF JAMES JOYCE, by Matthew J. C. Hodgart and Mabel P. Worthington; New York (1959)
—contains lists, useful for specialists, of all the songs Joyce quotes or mentions.

THE ART OF JAMES JOYCE, by Walton Litz (1961)
—a careful analysis of Joyce's methods of composition, based on years of study of the Joyce manuscripts.

THE CLASSICAL TEMPER, by S. L. Goldberg (1961)
—sees Joyce as a novelist in the classical manner.

JAMES JOYCE, by S. L. Goldberg (1962)
—a short general survey by a critic who disapproves of Joyce's linguistic experiments.

THE DUBLIN DIARY OF STANISLAUS JOYCE, ed. George Harris Healey (1962).

THE IRISH COMIC TRADITION, by Vivian Mercier (1962)
—sees Joyce as a great but typical figure in an ancient tradition.

EIGHT MODERN WRITERS, by J. I. M. Stewart; Oxford (1963).

FLAUBERT, JOYCE AND BECKETT: The Stoic Comedians, by Hugh Kenner (1964).

JAMES JOYCE, by A. Walton Litz; New York (1966)
—an up-to-date account of all Joyce's works, intended for American college students.

JAMES JOYCE TODAY, ed. Thomas F. Staley; Bloomington (1966)
—essays by various writers on Joyce's major works.

THE JOYCE PARADOX, by Arnold Goldman (1967)
—an analysis of Joyce's methods and philosophy with special reference to Kierkegaard.

JAMES JOYCE REMEMBERED, by C. P. Curran (1968)
—memories of a fellow-student of Joyce in Dublin and Paris.

JAMES JOYCE: The Critical Heritage, ed. R. H. Deming, 2 vols (1970)
—Vol. I, 1907–27; Vol. II, 1928–41. The two volumes contain over
300 articles, some abridged, from many countries and viewpoints.

DEAR MISS WEAVER by J. Lidderdale and M. Nicholson (1970)
—a portrait of Miss Harriet Weaver, founder of the Egoist Press
which published *Portrait of the Artist* and *Ulysses*; provides valuable
information on Joyce's early struggle for recognition and on the
encouragement and financial help he received from Miss Weaver.

(ii) *Studies of specific works*

Early works

TIME OF APPRENTICESHIP: The Fiction of Young James Joyce, by
Marvin Magalaner (1959)
—contains interesting notes on the factual bases of Joyce's stories, and
reproduces the first version of 'The Sisters'. The account of the
sources of 'The Dead' is most valuable.

A NEW APPROACH TO JOYCE: 'The Portrait of the Artist' as a Guide-
Book, by Rober S. Ryf; University of California (1962).

JOYCE'S 'PORTRAIT': Criticisms and Critiques, ed. Thomas Connolly;
New York (1962).

PORTRAITS OF AN ARTIST: A Casebook on Joyce's 'A Portrait', ed.
William E. Morris and Clifford A. Nault; New York (1962)
—these two books are excellent examples of the modern, and much
criticized, American 'casebook'. They provide the student with a
wide range of articles from learned periodicals and extracts from
full-length works, with full critical apparatus, and bibliographies.

JAMES JOYCE'S 'DUBLINERS': Critical Essays, ed. C. Hart (1969).

Ulysses

JAMES JOYCE'S 'ULYSSES', by Stuart Gilbert (1930)
—this work, slightly revised in 1952, gives an account of the Homeric
parallels and other structural features as explained by Joyce himself.

JAMES JOYCE AND THE MAKING OF 'ULYSSES', by Frank Budgen (1934)
—the best account of Joyce as a friend and writer.

WORD INDEX TO JOYCE'S 'ULYSSES', by M. L. Hanley and others:
Wisconsin (1937).

FABULOUS VOYAGER, by Richard M. Kain; Chicago (1947)
—complements Gilbert's book by giving the surface facts, such as
Joyce's use of newspapers and street plans and directories.

JOYCE AND SHAKESPEARE: A Study in the Meaning of 'Ulysses', by
William M. Schutte; Yale (1957).

SURFACE AND SYMBOL: The Consistency of James Joyce's 'Ulysses', by
Robert M. Adams; New York (1962).

THE ARGUMENT OF ULYSSES, by Stanley Sultan, Columbus; Ohio (1964)
—a thorough and illuminating account of the narrative of the novel.

THE BLOOMSDAY BOOK, by Harry Blamires (1966)
—a general guide book published in paperback.

Finnegans Wake

OUR EXAGMINATION ROUND HIS FACTIFICATION FOR INCAMINATION OF
WORK IN PROGRESS, by Samuel Beckett and others; Paris (1929)
—re-issued with additional material, 1961. Joyce said that he 'stood
behind' the twelve authors, presumably directing their work.

A SKELETON KEY TO FINNEGANS WAKE, by Joseph Campbell and Henry
Morton Robinson (1947)
—the gallant first attempt at a page by page explanation of Joyce's
book.

A CENSUS OF 'FINNEGANS WAKE', by Adaline Glasheen (1957)
—an alphabetical list of the characters, with other useful information.
The second, revised, edition, *A Second Census of Finnegans Wake*,
Evanston (1963) has many new entries.

THE BOOKS AT THE WAKE: A Study of Literary Allustions in James
Joyce's 'Finnegans Wake', by James S. Atherton (1959).

ANNA LIVIA PLURABELLE: The Making of a Chapter, by Fred H.
Higginson; Minneapolis (1960).

STRUCTURE AND MOTIV IN FINNEGANS WAKE, by Clive Hart; Minneapolis
(1963).

A CONCORDANCE TO FINNEGANS WAKE, by Clive Hart; Minneapolis
(1963).

TWELVE AND A TILLY, ed. Jack P. Dalton and Clive Hart (1966)
—essays for the twenty-fifth anniversary of *Finnegans Wake*.

ETERNAL GEOMATER: The Sexual Universe of 'Finnegans Wake',
by M. C. Solomon; Carbondale (1969)
—contains an interesting chapter on non-Euclidean geometry in
Finnegans Wake.

A READER'S GUIDE TO 'FINNEGANS WAKE', by W. Y. Tindall (1969)
—a report on twenty years' study at Columbia University.

(iii) *Some Articles and Reviews*

'Dubliners and Mr James Joyce', by Ezra Pound, *The Egoist*, i, 14,
15 July 1914.

'Joyce', by E. Pound, *The Future*, May 1918.

'*Ulysses*', by E. Pound, *The Dial*, LXXII, No. 6, June 1922
—these three essays are reprinted in *Literary Essays of Ezra Pound*, ed.
T. S. Eliot, 1954.

'James Joyce', by Valéry Larbaud, *Nouvelle revue française*, XXIV,
April, 1922
—English translation in *Criterion*, I, October 1922. The first explanation
of the structure of *Ulysses*.

'The Position of Joyce', by Cyril Connolly, *Life and Letters*, April 1929
—reprinted in *The Condemned Playground*, by C. Connolly (1945).

'*Ulysses*: Ein Monolog', by C. G. Jung, *Europäische revue*, VII, 1932
—English translation in *Nimbus*, ii, 1953.

'Joyce and the Eighteenth-Century Novelists', by G. Melchiori,
English Miscellany, 2, ed. Mario Praz (1951).

Envoy: An Irish Review of Literature and Art, V, April 1951
—contains several shrewd and amusing articles in a special Joyce
number.

'Shakespeare and *Finnegans Wake*', by M. J. C. Hodgart, *Cambridge
Journal*, VI, September 1953.

'*Finnegans Wake* and the Girls from Boston, Mass.', by Adaline
Glasheen, *Hudson Review*, VII, i, Spring 1955.

'*Finnegans Wake*: the Gist of the Pantomime', by J. S. Atherton,
Accent, XV, i, Winter 1955.

'From *Finnegans Wake*: a Sentence in Progress', by David Hayman,
PMLA, LXXIII, i, March 1958
—a careful study of thirteen stages in Joyce's composition of a
sentence.

'The Characteristics of Leopold Bloom', by Joseph Prescott, *Literature and Psychology*, IV, i, Winter 1959.

'Some Zürich Allusions in *Finnegans Wake*', by Fritz Senn, *The Analyst*, XIX, December 1960
—a thorough account by a native of Zurich.

'James Joyce: Unfacts, Fiction, and Facts', by William T. Noon, S.J., *PMLA*, LXXVI, i, June 1961
—an urbane attempt to settle the vexed question of Joyce's attitude to religion.

'Joyce's Letters and His Use of "Place,"' by Chester Anderson, *James Joyce Quarterly*, IV, ii, Winter, 1967
—an informative review of Joyce's *Letters*.

'The Non-information of Finnegan's Wake', by Denis Johnston. *The Massachussetts Review*, Winter 1964
—this entire issue was devoted to writers of twentieth-century Ireland.

Note: Interpretation of Joyce's work is being attempted in many places and several periodicals have been devoted entirely to this task.

The James Joyce Review, New York, edited by Edgar Epstein, appeared in four quarterly numbers in 1957, and as a single 'double-number' in 1958, and again in 1959, when it ceased publication. Several important articles were published in it.

The Analyst, edited by Robert Mayo, is published occasionally by the Department of English of Northwestern University. It has devoted many issues entirely to Joyce and published articles, sometimes very lengthy, by John V. Kelleher, Adaline Glasheen, Fritz Senn, and others.

A Wake Newslitter, edited by Clive Hart and Fritz Senn, is now sponsored by the English Department of the University of Dundee. Its first 18 numbers (from March 1962 to March 1964) which had no official support, contained articles by Thornton Wilder, M. J. C. Hodgart, Adaline Glasheen, Nathan Halper, the editors, and many others.

The James Joyce Quarterly, University of Tulsa, Oklahoma, is edited by Thomas F. Staley, and has been appearing since the autumn of 1963.